WITHDRAWN

THE NUMBER SYSTEM AND COMMON AND DECIMAL FRACTIONS

THE NUMBER SYSTEM AND COMMON AND DECIMAL FRACTIONS

EDITED BY MICHAEL J. COMINSKEY

Britannica®
Educational Publishing

IN ASSOCIATION WITH

ROSEN
EDUCATIONAL SERVICES

Published in 2015 by Britannica Educational Publishing (a trademark of Encyclopædia Britannica, Inc.) in association with The Rosen Publishing Group, Inc.
29 East 21st Street, New York, NY 10010

Distributed exclusively by Rosen Publishing.
To see additional Britannica Educational Publishing titles, go to rosenpublishing.com

First Edition

Britannica Educational Publishing
J. E. Luebering: Director, Core Reference Group
Anthony L. Green: Editor, Compton's by Britannica

Rosen Publishing
Hope Lourie Killcoyne: Executive Editor
Michael J. Cominskey: Editor
Nelson Sá: Art Director
Nicole Russo: Designer
Cindy Reiman: Photography Manager
Introduction and conclusion by John Strazzabosco

Cataloging-in-Publication Data

YA
513.5 C

The number system and common and decimal fractions/edited by Michael J. Cominskey.—First edition.
    pages cm.—(The story of math : core principles of mathematics)
Includes bibliographical references and index.
ISBN 978-1-62275-524-0 (library bound)
1. Numerals—Juvenile literature. 2. Numeration—Juvenile literature. 3. Fractions—Juvenile literature.
I. Cominskey, Michael J., editor.   11/15
QA141.3.N83 2015   Sebco
513.5—dc23   31.70

2014024516

Manufactured in the United States of America

Contents

Introduction

I magine being a Roman citizen confronted with a math problem 2,000 years ago. In the days of ancient Rome, if a merchant or tax collector needed to calculate thirteen plus sixty-nine, he would use pebbles or metal disks as counters. Romans moved these pebbles on marked boards to work out problems. Later the counters were strung on wires mounted in a frame.

People used this device—called an abacus—instead of working out their problems in writing because they could not "carry ten" conveniently with their cumbersome system of writing numbers. The Roman numeral system, in which letters represent numbers, was dominant in Europe for nearly 2,000 years. However, even simple addition of Roman numerals—in our example, XIII + LXIX—was difficult.

The math world made a great advancement when the Hindu-Arabic numeral system simplified matters several hundred years later by replacing a cumbersome XXIV with the sleek expression 24. In math, efficiency is key. With a simplified decimal system of numeration, mathematicians could now concentrate on depth and meaningful discovery in the field

Ancient Roman merchants and tax collectors calculated math problems using a device called an abacus, such as the one shown here. Science & Society Picture Library/Getty Images

of mathematics, and mathematicians would of course find the new Hindu-Arabic numerals easier to read and write.

In this text, the reader will be pulled into the world of how we conceive of, count, and write numbers, explaining both the importance and practical applications of each number system presented.

Today's student might remark, "But calculators and computers yield exact computations for us." This is true. But the computer must first be programmed, or told how to perform. The number system that calculators and computers use is what is called a binary system, which might be a new concept for the reader. As explained in this book, an understanding of the underlying basis of modern mathematical tools—including the binary system—will enhance the reader's skills in using both the tools and the math.

Does this suggest that, for instance, the decimal system that the math student is familiar with must now be tossed out? The answer, of course, is no. The reader will also find new ways to explore those systems with which he or she is already quite familiar. Lucid and captivating explanations will enhance understanding of the number systems underlying all mathematics, such as techniques for converting from one base system to another, applications of various base systems, conversion of common fractions into decimal fractions, and conversion of decimals back into common fractions.

Included are hints and practice problems that make the mastery of these techniques easier to accomplish. Each example is shown with a simple illustration, without which the reader might easily fall into little errors and traps that could make the calculation frustrating.

When asked to add mixed fractions, even the best of math students might be initially stumped for lack of just a single hint that would get the whole process started. This book of number systems, decimals, and fractions—and the many techniques it explains—is therefore a handy tool for any middle or high school student (or his or her parent) to have on the shelf for both problem solving and historical reference.

NUMERATION SYSTEMS

More than 5,000 years ago an Egyptian ruler recorded, perhaps with a bit of exaggeration, the capture of 120,000 prisoners, 400,000 oxen, and 1,422,000 goats. This event was inscribed on a ceremonial mace, or club, that is now in a museum in Oxford, England.

The ancient Egyptians developed the art of counting to a high degree, but their system of numeration was very crude. For example, the number 1,000 was symbolized by a picture of a lotus flower, and the number 2,000 was symbolized by a picture of two lotus flowers growing out of a bush. Although these symbols, called hieroglyphics, permitted the Egyptians to write large numbers, the numeration system was clumsy and awkward to work with. The number 999, for instance, required 27 individual marks.

King Narmer of ancient Egypt (pictured above) *recorded great military feats and the capture of prisoners on maces and palettes. He exaggerated these figures using hieroglyphics that represented very large numbers.* Hirmer Fotoarchiv, Munich

In our system of numeration, we use ten symbols called digits—0, 1, 2, 3, 4, 5, 6, 7, 8, and 9—and combinations of these symbols. Our system of numeration is called the decimal, or base-ten, system. There is little doubt that our ten fingers influenced the development of a numeration system based on ten digits.

Other numeration systems were developed in early cultures and societies. Two of the most common were the base-five system, related to the number of fingers on one hand, and the base-twenty system, related to the number of fingers and toes.

In some languages the word for "five" is the same as the word for "hand," and the word for "ten" is the same as the word for "two hands." In our own language the word "digit" is a synonym for the word "finger"—that is, ten digits, ten fingers.

Still another early system of numeration was a base-sixty system developed by the Mesopotamians and used for centuries. These ancient people divided the year into 360 days (6 × 60). To this day we still divide the hour into 60 minutes and the minute into 60 seconds. Numeration systems of current interest include a binary, or base-two, system used in computers and a base-twelve, or duo-decimal, system.

It is worthwhile for everyone to become familiar with the principles of the base-twelve system of numeration and with those of base-two, base-five, or other systems. Working with other bases gives deeper insight into the decimal system that most people in the modern world have used since childhood. Before considering other systems, however, let us investigate our more familiar decimal system.

THE DECIMAL SYSTEM

The ten digits of our numeration system are used to name the numbers of dots shown in these frames:

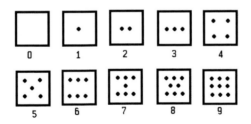

If we were not familiar with our system of numeration, a reasonable method for naming the number of dots in frames showing 10, 11, and 12 dots might be somewhat as follows:

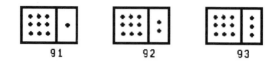

91   92   93

A system of numeration based on such a procedure as this is called an additive, or sign-value, system. The numeral 995 would represent the sum 9 + 9 + 5. In an additive system of numeration, the value of each numeral is the equivalent of the sum of its individual numeric signs or digits. However, in our system of numeration, we use a positional, or place-value, system invented by ancient Hindu mathematicians. The positional system of numeration has many advantages over a simple additive system.

In a positional system of numeration, the value assigned to a digit depends upon its position in the numeral. For example, in our decimal positional system the 1 in the numeral 103 refers to one group of 100; the 0 refers to zero groups of 10; and the 3 refers to three 1s.

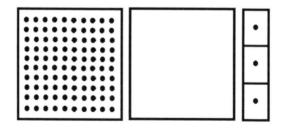

103 = [1 X (10 X 10)] + [0 X (10)] + [3 X (1)]

The symbol 10^2 is a convenient shorthand notation for the product of 10 × 10. The symbol ^{2} is called an exponent, and it tells you that 10 is to be multiplied by itself. In the same notation,

$$10 \times 10 \times 10 = 10^3 \text{ and } 10 \times 10 \times 10 \times 10 = 10^4.$$

Using this shorthand notation, the numeral 1,572 can be expressed:

$$1{,}572 = [1 \times 10^3] + [5 \times 10^2] + [7 \times 10] + [2 \times 1].$$

Numbers such as 1, 6, 230, and 1,572 are called whole numbers. The ten digits may be used to represent not only whole numbers but also numbers less than one and numbers which are sums of whole numbers and numbers less than one. These numbers can be represented either as fractions or as decimals. The value assigned to each digit is again determined by its position in the numeral. For example:

$$.132 = \left[1 \times \frac{1}{10}\right] + \left[3 \times \frac{1}{100}\right] + \left[2 \times \frac{1}{1000}\right], \quad \text{and}$$

$$23.35 = [2 \times 10] + [3 \times 1] + \left[3 \times \frac{1}{10}\right] + \left[5 \times \frac{1}{100}\right]$$

Common and decimal fractions will be discussed in more depth in later sections of this book.

BASE–FIVE NUMERATION SYSTEM

Now, consider a frame with 17 dots, thinking of it in terms of one group of 10 dots and 7 more dots:

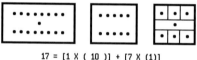

17 = [1 X (10)] + [7 X (1)]

This matches our understanding of the number 17 in the decimal system. But we may also think of it as three groups of 5 dots and 2 more dots:

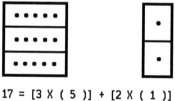

17 = [3 X (5)] + [2 X (1)]

The numeral 32_{five} is a shorthand notation for $[3 \times (5)] + [2 \times (1)]$. The subscript "five" tells you that the numeral is expressed in the base-five, or quinary, system of numeration. In the base-five system of numeration, just five digits are used: 0, 1, 2, 3, and 4. While not particularly common, the quinary system is used in certain Austronesian languages, as well as by speakers of Saraveca, a South American Arawak language. In our discussion a numeral without a subscript is considered to be base-ten. Thus,

$$17 = [1 \times (10)] + [7 \times (1)] = [3 \times (5)] + [2 \times (1)]$$
$$= 32_{\text{five}}.$$

Similarly, the numeral 214_{five} represents

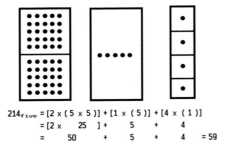

$$214_{\text{five}} = [2 \times (5 \times 5)] + [1 \times (5)] + [4 \times (1)]$$
$$= [2 \times \quad 25 \quad] + \quad 5 \quad + \quad 4$$
$$= \quad 50 \quad + \quad 5 \quad + \quad 4 \quad = 59$$

An easy way to recognize the significance and meaning of positional, or place, value and the relationship between base-ten and base-five is to think about the ways in which we express amounts of money. In the base-ten system you may think about pennies (units), dimes (tens), and dollars (hundreds), depending upon the position of the digit in the numeral. Similarly, in the base-five system you may think about pennies (units), nickels (fives), and quarters (twenty-fives).

For example, 431_{five} (cents) may be exchanged for

4 (quarters) + 3 (nickels) + 1 (cent).

In turn, this may be exchanged for

1 (dollar) + 1 (dime) + 6 (cents),

which may be exchanged for 116 (cents). Thus, $431_{five} = 116_{ten}$.

THE BINARY SYSTEM

Consider a frame with seven dots. Instead of thinking in terms of groups of ten or groups of five, we may think in terms of groups of two:

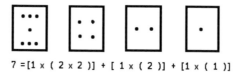

$$7 = [1 \times (2 \times 2)] + [1 \times (2)] + [1 \times (1)]$$

The numeral 111_{two} is a shorthand notation for

NUMERALS				Base-Two
Base-Ten	Base-Two			Base-Two
0	0_{two}	=	$[0 \times (1)] = 0$	0_{two}
1	1_{two}	=	$[1 \times (1)] = 1$	1_{two}
2	10_{two}	=	$[1 \times (2)] + [0 \times (1)] = 2$	10_{two}
3	11_{two}	=	$[1 \times (2)] + [1 \times (1)] = 2 + 1 = 3$	11_{two}
4	100_{two}	=	$[1 \times (2 \times 2)] + [0 \times (2)] + [0 \times (1)] = 4 + 0 + 0 = 4$	100_{two}
7	111_{two}	=	$[1 \times (2 \times 2)] + [1 \times (2)] + [1 \times (1)] = 4 + 2 + 1 = 7$	111_{two}
8	1000_{two}	=	$[1 \times (2 \times 2 \times 2)] + [0 \times (2 \times 2)] + [0 \times (2)] + [0 \times (1)] = 8$	1000_{two}
16	10000_{two}	=	$[1 \times (2 \times 2 \times 2 \times 2)] + 0 + 0 + 0 + 0 = 16$	10000_{two}
19	10011_{two}	=	$[1 \times (2 \times 2 \times 2 \times 2)] + 0 + 0 + [1 \times (2)] + [1 \times (1)] = 16+0+0+2+1 = 19$	10011_{two}

Comparison of numerals in the base-ten and base-two systems.
Encyclopædia Britannica, Inc.

$$[1 \times (2 \times 2)] + [1 \times (2)] + [1 \times (1)].$$

The subscript "two" tells you that the numeral is expressed in the base-two system of numeration. In this system only two digits—0 and 1—are used.

Let us see how one would do arithmetic problems in the binary system.

Addition				Multiplication		
0	1	1		0	1	1
+0	+0	+1		x0	x0	x1
0	1	10		0	0	1

The simplicity of binary arithmetic makes the binary system well suited for use in computers. The importance of the binary system to information theory and computer technology derives mainly from the compact and reliable manner in which

One of the primary uses of the binary system today is in information theory and computer technology due to its compact, simple notation of large amounts of data. JMiks/Shutterstock.com

0s and 1s can be represented in electro-mechanical devices with two states—such as "on-off," "open-closed," or "go–no go." The digit 1, for instance, may correspond to a light turned on, and the digit 0 to a light turned off. In this scheme, the number 10110_{two} may correspond to this arrangement of lights:

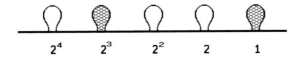

THE DUODECIMAL SYSTEM

Consider a frame with 30 dots. We may consider groups of 12:

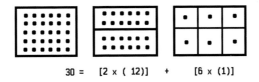

$$30 = [2 \times (12)] + [6 \times (1)]$$

The numeral 26_{twelve} is a shorthand notation for

$$[2 \times (12)] + [6 \times (1)].$$

The subscript "twelve" tells you that the numeral is expressed in the base-twelve, or duodecimal, system of numeration. While we are mostly familiar with measurements making use of the decimal system today, the duodecimal system will still be familiar to most readers due to its many remnants in contemporary culture. Thus, 12 occurs as the number of inches in a foot, months in a year, ounces in a pound, and twice 12 hours in a day, and both the dozen and the gross measure by twelves.

The base-twelve system requires 12 symbols, so we shall use the 10 digits and the letters X and E.

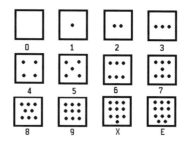

Thus,

$$9_{twelve} = 9 \times (1) = 9$$
$$X_{twelve} = X \times (1) = 10 \times (1) = 10$$
$$E_{twelve} = E \times (1) = 11 \times (1) = 11$$
$$10_{twelve} = [1 \times (12)] + [0 \times (1)] = 12 + 0 = 12$$
$$1X_{twelve} = [1 \times (12)] + [X \times (1)]$$
$$= [1 \times (12)] + [10 \times (1)] = 12 + 10 = 22$$
$$EXO_{twelve} = [E \times (12 \times 12)] + [X \times (12)] + [0 \times (1)]$$
$$= [11 \times (12 \times 12)] + [10 \times 12] +$$
$$= \quad\quad 1584 \quad + \quad 120 \quad\quad\quad = 1704$$

CONVERTING FROM ONE BASE TO ANOTHER

You already know how to convert base-two, base-five, and base-twelve numerals into base-ten numerals. Now, using the idea of place value, you can easily convert a numeral of any given base to a base-ten numeral. For example:

$$37_{eight} = [3 \times (8)] + [7 \times (1)] = 24 + 7 = 31$$

$$146_{seven} = 01 \times (7 \times 7)] + [4 \times (7)] + [6 \times (1)] = 49 + 28 + 6 = 83$$

It may require a little more thought to convert a base-ten numeral into a numeral of another base. The following examples show how you can apply the principles of place value to convert from base-ten to another base.

EXAMPLE I

Suppose that you wish to convert the base-ten numeral 19 into a base-two numeral. First notice that

```
2 X 2 X 2 X 2 ( =16 ) is less than 19,
and 19 is less than 2 X 2 X 2 X 2 X 2 ( =32 ).
                19
Subtract: − 16
                 3  So, 19 = [1 X (2 X 2 X 2 X 2)] + 3.
Now notice that
                3 = [1 X (2)] + [1 X (1)].

So, 19 = [1 X (2 X 2 X 2 X 2)] + [0 X (2 X 2 X 2)]
   + [0 X (2 X 2)] + [1 X (2)] + [1 X (1)] = 10011 two
```

EXAMPLE 2

Convert the base–ten numeral 67 into a base–five numeral. Notice that

5 X 5 (= 25) is less than 67
and 67 is less than 5 X 5 X 5 (= 125).

Now substract:
$$\begin{array}{r} 67 \\ -25 \\ \hline 42 \end{array}$$

Subtract again:
$$\begin{array}{r} -25 \\ \hline 17 \end{array}$$ So, 67 = [2 X (5 X 5)] + 17.

Now notice that
5 is less than 17,
and 17 is less than 5 X 5 (= 25).

Subtract:
$$\begin{array}{r} 17 \\ -5 \\ \hline 12 \end{array}$$

Subtract again:
$$\begin{array}{r} -5 \\ \hline 7 \end{array}$$

Subtract again:
$$\begin{array}{r} -5 \\ \hline 2 \end{array}$$ So, 17 = [3 X (5)] + 2,

and 67 = [2 x (5 x 5)] + [3 X (5)] + [2 X (1)] = 232 five.

EXAMPLE 3

Convert the base–ten numeral 587 into a base–twelve numeral. Notice that

12 X 12(= 144) is less than 587,
and 587 is less than 12 X 12 x 12 (= 1728).

Divide:
$$\begin{array}{r} 4 \\ 144 \overline{)587} \\ 576 \\ \hline 11 \end{array}$$ So, 587 = [4 X (12 X 12)] + 11.

Recall that 11 = E twelve.

So, 587 = [4 X (12 X 12)] + [0 X (12)]
+ [E X 1] = 40 E twelve.

When working with base-twelve, it may be helpful to think about units, dozens, and gross (144, or 12 × 12). For example, 431_{twelve} (units) is the same as

4 (gross) + 3 (dozen) + 1 (unit).

In turn, this is the same as

$[4 × (12 × 12)]$ (units) + $[3 × (12)]$ (units) + $[1 × (1)]$ (units),

which is the same as 613 units. Thus, 431_{twelve} = 613.

You may also think about inches and feet. For example, XE_{twelve} (inches) is the same as

X (feet) + E (inches), or 10 (feet) + 11 (inches).

This is the same as 131 (inches). Thus, XE_{twelve} = 131.

Following are some base-twelve addition problems with related examples shown alongside.

27	2 ft. 7 in.	428	4 gr. 2 doz. 8 un.
+3E	+3 ft. 11 in.	+ XE	+ 10 doz. 11 un.
66	6 ft. 6 in.	517	5 gr. 1 doz. 7 un.

NUMERAL SYSTEMS

Numeral systems are sets of symbols and the rules for using them to represent numbers, which are used to express how many objects are in a given set. Thus the idea of "oneness" can be represented by the Roman numeral I, by the Greek letter alpha α (the first letter) used as a numeral, by the Hebrew letter aleph א (the first letter) used as a numeral, or by the modern numeral 1, which is Hindu-Arabic in origin.

THE ADOPTION OF PLACE-VALUE SYSTEMS

Very likely the earliest system of written symbols in ancient Mesopotamia was a system of symbols for numbers. Modern numeral systems are place-value systems—that is, the value of the symbol depends upon the position or place of the symbol in the representation; for example, the 2 in 20 and 200 represents two tens and two hundreds, respectively. Most ancient systems, such as the Egyptian, Roman, Hebrew, and Greek numeral systems, did not have a positional characteristic, and this complicated arithmetical calculations.

While most ancient systems lacked this positional characteristic, other systems—including the Babylonian, one version each of the Chinese and Indian, as well as the Mayan system—did employ the principle of place value. As

This ancient Babylonian clay tablet shows mathematical problems in cuneiform—a reminder of one of the earliest written numeral systems to employ the principle of place value. Print Collector/Hulton Archive/ Getty Images

previously mentioned, the most commonly used numeral system today is the decimal-positional numeral system, the decimal referring to the use of 10 symbols—0, 1, 2, 3, 4, 5, 6, 7, 8, 9—to construct all numbers. This was an invention of the Indians, perfected in the medieval Islamic world. Because this system was translated into Arabic prior to its introduction into Europe by traveling merchants around the 13th century, it is commonly known as the Hindu-Arabic system.

The two other common positional systems are used in computers and computing science, namely the aforementioned binary system, with its two symbols—0 and 1—and a hexadecimal, or base-sixteen, system, with 16 symbols—0, 1, 2,..., 9, A, B,..., F.

ROMAN NUMERALS AND THE MIDDLE AGES

Adoption of the Hindu-Arabic system met resistance due to the widespread use of the Roman numeral system during the 13th century when it was introduced to Europe. The Roman numeral system, in which letters represent numbers, was dominant in Europe for nearly 2,000 years. Roman numerals are hard to manipulate, however, and mathematical calculations generally were done on an abacus. As the fortunes of the Roman Empire declined, however, a rising interest in mathematics developed elsewhere, in India and among Arab scholars. Gradually, the superior Hindu-Arabic system was learned by the Europeans, and eventually it replaced the Roman system.

COMPUTATIONS IN ROMAN AND HINDU-ARABIC NUMERALS

The Roman system, like others that are not based on the principle of position, does not provide an efficient and easy method of computation. This led to its gradual replacement by more useful place–value systems, such as the decimal or binary systems. Here are some examples of computations using the Roman system. Equivalent computations using the Hindu–Arabic system are alongside.

$$
\begin{array}{r} IV \\ + III \\ \hline VII \end{array} \quad \begin{array}{r} 4 \\ + 3 \\ \hline 7 \end{array} \qquad \begin{array}{r} XXXII \\ - XVIII \\ \hline XIV \end{array} \quad \begin{array}{r} 32 \\ - 18 \\ \hline 14 \end{array}
$$

$$
\begin{array}{r} XII \\ \times \quad III \\ \hline XXXVI \end{array} \quad \begin{array}{r} 12 \\ \times 3 \\ \hline 36 \end{array} \qquad \frac{LXIV}{IV} = XVI \qquad \frac{64}{4} = 16
$$

Indian mathematicians were especially skilled in arithmetic, methods of calculation, algebra, and trigonometry. Aryabhata calculated pi to a very accurate value of 3.1416, and Brahmagupta and Bhaskara II advanced the study of indeterminate equations. Because Indian mathematicians were not concerned with such theoretical problems as irrational numbers, they were able to make great strides in algebra. Their decimal place-valued number system, including zero, was especially suited for easy calculation. Indian mathematicians, however, lacked interest in a sense of proof. Most of their results were presented simply as useful techniques for given situations, especially in astronomical or astrological computations.

One of the greatest scientific minds of Islam was al-Khwarizmi, who introduced the name (*al-jabr*) that became known as algebra. Consequently, the numbers familiar to most people are still referred to as Arabic numerals. Arab mathematicians also translated and commented on Ptolemy's astronomy before it was brought to the attention of Europeans. Islamic scholars not only translated the works of Euclid, Archimedes,

Aryabhata (476–550? CE) was an important Indian mathematician and astronomer who made an early calculation of the value of pi to four decimal places. Sheila Terry/Science Source

Apollonius, and Ptolemy into Arabic but advanced beyond what the Greek mathematicians had done to provide new results of their own.

Roman numerals can still be seen to this day on the faces of clocks, in the front matter of books, and often simply for decorative purposes.
Mircea Maties/Shutterstock.com

By the end of the 8th century the influence of Islam had extended as far west as Spain. It was there, primarily, that Arabic, Jewish, and Western scholars eventually translated Greek and Islamic manuscripts into Latin. By the 13th century, original mathematical work by European authors had begun to appear.

Despite being replaced in mathematics by the Hindu-Arabic numeral system, Roman numerals are still sometimes used today. Some examples of items on or in which Roman numerals still appear include clock faces and books, for numbering introductory pages and chapters.

THE REAL NUMBERS

A numeration system provides the numerals by which we may name numbers. Now, let us use our decimal system of numeration to study the set of real numbers.

When we say that a man is 6 feet tall, weighs 180 pounds, and is 30 years old, we are using numbers as measures of magnitudes. Numbers that are used in this way may be referred to as numbers-of-arithmetic.

Numbers that are used as measures of directed change are called real numbers. For example, if we are speaking about temperature, a five-degree increase in temperature may be measured by the real number +5 (said "positive five"), while a five-degree decrease in temperature may be measured by the real number −5 (said "negative five"). The set of real numbers consists of all the positive numbers, all the negative numbers,

Real numbers are numbers used as measures of directed change, such as the increase or decrease in the temperature measured by a thermometer.
Dora Zett/Shutterstock.com

and zero. The number-of-arithmetic o corresponds to the real number o.

Corresponding to each nonzero number-of-arithmetic—that is, to each number-of-arithmetic other than o—there are exactly two real numbers. For example, corresponding to the number-of-arithmetic 5 there are exactly two real numbers: +5 and ⁻5. The number-of-arithmetic 5 is called the arithmetic value of the real numbers +5 and ⁻5.

OPERATIONS ON REAL NUMBERS

The sum of a pair of real numbers is a measure of the resultant of a pair of directed changes. For example, if the temperature increases by 5 degrees and later decreases by 3 degrees, the resultant change would be an increase of 2 degrees. The sum +5 + ⁻3 is the same as +2. For short,

+5 + ⁻3 = +2.

A decrease of 5 degrees followed by an increase of 3 degrees would result in a decrease of 2 degrees:

⁻5 + +3 = ⁻2.

A decrease of 5 degrees followed by another decrease of 3 degrees would result in a decrease of 8 degrees:

$$-5 + -3 = -8.$$

Thinking of real numbers as measures of directed change also motivates rules for multiplying the real numbers. Let us suppose, for example, that the temperature on January 1 is 0 degrees. If the temperature then increases 5 degrees per day, the resultant change in temperature 3 days later is an increase of 15 degrees:

$$+5 \times +3 = +15.$$

Rule: The product of a positive number multiplied by a positive number is a positive number.

If the temperature decreases 5 degrees per day, the resultant change in temperature 3 days later is a decrease of 15 degrees:

$$-5 \times +3 = -15.$$

Rule: The product of a negative number multiplied by a positive number is a negative number.

Suppose that the temperature had been decreasing 5 degrees per day for the past 3 days. Then 3 days earlier the temperature was 15 degrees higher:

$$-5 \times -3 = +15.$$

Rule: The product of a negative number multiplied by a negative number is a positive number.

Notice that operations on real numbers correspond in a natural way with operations on their arithmetic values. The arithmetic value of a positive real number is often written as an abbreviation for the real number.

Some Operations on Real Numbers			Some Operations on Numbers-of-Arithmetic
$\begin{array}{r} +8 \\ +\ +4 \\ \hline +12 \end{array}$	$\begin{array}{r} -8 \\ +\ -4 \\ \hline -12 \end{array}$		$\begin{array}{r} 8 \\ +\ 4 \\ \hline 12 \end{array}$
$\begin{array}{r} +8 \\ +\ -4 \\ \hline +4 \end{array}$	$\begin{array}{r} -8 \\ +\ +4 \\ \hline -4 \end{array}$		$\begin{array}{r} 8 \\ -\ 4 \\ \hline 4 \end{array}$
$\begin{array}{r} +8 \\ X\ +4 \\ \hline +32 \end{array}$	$\begin{array}{r} +8 \\ X\ -4 \\ \hline +32 \end{array}$	$\begin{array}{r} -8 \\ X\ -4 \\ \hline +32 \end{array}$	$\begin{array}{r} 8 \\ X\ 4 \\ \hline 32 \end{array}$

THE NUMBER LINE

The set of real numbers may be pictured as the set of points on a line, and we speak of the set of real numbers as the number line. A point on the line is chosen to represent the number 0, and other points are chosen for the numbers +1, +2, +3, +4, and so on.

The set of positive integers is called a subset of the set of real numbers and consists of all the positive numbers. The set of negative integers is also a subset of the set of real numbers and consists of all the negative numbers: −1, −2, −3, −4, and so on.

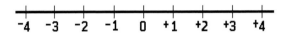

The drawing of the number line may be extended to the right and to the left as necessary. The set of integers consists of all the positive integers, all the negative integers, and zero.

RATIONAL AND IRRATIONAL NUMBERS

When one integer is divided by another non-zero integer, the quotient is called a rational number. Rational numbers may be represented as fractions.

For example, the fraction $^{+1}/_{+2}$ represents the quotient of +1 divided by +2. The symbol above the line is called the numerator, and the symbol below the line is called the denominator.

Rational numbers may also be represented as decimals. A fraction can be converted by division to the decimal representation as follows:

$$\frac{+1}{+2} = +.5 \qquad 2)\overline{\begin{array}{c} .5 \\ 1.0 \\ \underline{1\ 0} \\ 0 \end{array}} \qquad \frac{-3}{+5} = -.6 \qquad 5)\overline{\begin{array}{c} .6 \\ 3.0 \\ \underline{3\ 0} \\ 0 \end{array}}$$

You may have noticed that the rational numbers include both positive and negative integers. For example, −4 is a rational number because $^{-4}/_{+1} = -4$.

In the real-number system, every rational number corresponds to a point on the number line. For example, the point corresponding to $+(^7/_3)$ may be found by dividing the segment between 0 and +1 into thirds and then constructing the segment 7 times as long as the segment from 0 to $+(^1/_3)$.

However, not every point that can be shown on a real-number line designates a rational number. The ancient Greek geometers were the first to discover that there are some real numbers that are not rational. They showed that if we construct a square measuring 1 unit by 1 unit, the length of the diagonal (denoted by *d* in the drawing) is not a rational number.

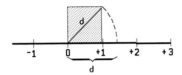

The Pythagorean Theorem, named after the Greek geometer Pythagoras, states that the square of the hypotenuse of a right triangle (or the side of the triangle oppo- site its right angle) is equal to the sum of the squares of the legs. By this theorem,

$$d^2 = 1^2 + 1^2 = 1 + 1 = 2.$$
So, $d = \sqrt{2}$.

The real numbers that are not rational are called irrational

The Greek mathematician Pythagoras (c. 570 BCE–c. 500–490 BCE) demonstrates the Pythagorean theorem with a stick in the sand.
© Photos.com/Thinkstock

PYTHAGORAS

The man who played a crucial role in formulating principles that influenced Plato and Aristotle was the Greek philosopher and mathematician Pythagoras. He founded the Pythagorean brotherhood, a group of followers whose beliefs and ideas were rediscovered during the Renaissance and contributed to the development of mathematics and Western rational philosophy.

Pythagoras was born in about 580 BCE on the island of Samos, in the Aegean Sea. It is said he spent his early years traveling widely in search of wisdom. He settled in Crotona, a Greek colony in southern Italy, about 530 BCE. A brotherhood of disciples soon gathered around him, inspired by his teachings. The group was strongly religious and devoted to reformation of political, moral, and social life. The order was influential in the region, but eventually its involvement in politics resulted in suppression of the brotherhood. Pythagoras was forced to retire and leave the area. He went to Metapontum, a Greek city in southern Italy. He died there in about 500 BCE.

Because none of the writings of Pythagoras have survived, it is difficult to distinguish his teachings from those of his disciples. Among the basic tenets of the Pythagoreans is the belief that reality, at its deepest level, is mathematical in nature.

numbers. Other irrational numbers are √3, √5, and π. (Said "square root of three," "square root of five," and "pi." Pi is the circumference of a circle whose diameter is 1 unit in length.)

The decimal of a rational number obtained by dividing an integer by a nonzero integer either terminates or is an infinite decimal which repeats a certain pattern. For example:

1/5 = .2 terminates; but 2/7 = .28571428571 4285714...repeats.

An irrational number cannot be obtained by dividing an integer by a nonzero integer. The decimal representation of an irrational number does not terminate, nor does it repeat a certain pattern. In the case of π:

π = 3.141592653589793238462643383279502884...

Recently, an approximation of π has been calculated to more than 2,700,000,000,000 decimal places by the use of computers.

COMMON AND DECIMAL FRACTIONS

There are many ways to make change for a dollar: two half-dollars, four quarters, ten dimes, 20 nickels, or 100 pennies. No matter how the change is made, the dollar is broken up—"fractured"—into several pieces. These pieces are called fractions, from the same Latin word (*fractus*, meaning "broken") from which the word "fracture" comes.

All fractions represent parts of a whole. It has long been convenient and customary to divide things into segments. Hours are divided into 60 minutes each. Days are divided into 24 hours, and years into 12 months. Miles are divided into feet, and kilometers into meters. Each of these segments can be expressed as a fraction. One inch is one twelve part, or one-twelfth, of a foot. Fractions are very helpful because they make

An easy way to think of fractions, or parts of a whole, is with the change that can make up a dollar. The above change amounts to 41 cents, or .41 of a dollar. Vlue/Shutterstock.com

possible measurements in quantities other than whole numbers, such as 1, 2, or 5. Measurements with fractions can also often be more precise: it is more exact to say "four and one-tenth gallons" than "a little more than four gallons."

TYPES OF FRACTIONS

In everyday mathematics there are two types of fractions, common and decimal. The only difference between the two is in how they are written. All fractions are written using the same symbols used to write whole numbers, but the symbols are used in a different way. Common fractions are written as $^4/_{10}$ or $^7/_{100}$: four over ten and seven over one hundred. The same numbers, when appearing as decimal fractions, would be 0.4 and 0.07. These would usually be read as "point four" and "point zero seven." They express the same amounts.

In a common fraction, the number below the line is the denominator, and the number above the line is the numerator. In reading a common fraction, the numerator is stated first. Thus, $^2/_3$ is read as two-thirds. Any number except zero can be either a denominator or a numerator. What is expressed in a common fraction is not only a quantity but also a ratio: the relationship of one quantity to another. For example, the fraction $^1/_2$ expresses the ratio of one to two: The relationship of one to two is that one is half of two. There are many common uses of ratios. When a baker makes a cake, he may use two cups of sugar for every three cups of flour: The ratio is two to three, and it may be expressed as a fraction, $^2/_3$.

Decimal fractions are so called because they are based on the decimal, or base-ten, numbering system. Sometimes referred to simply as "decimals," all decimal fractions consist of one

One practical use of ratios is in baking. When a baker changes the measurement of one ingredient, he must increase or decrease the other ingredients at the same ratio. area381/iStock/Thinkstock

or more numbers preceded by a dot called the decimal point: 0.4, for example, is read as four-tenths. If there is only one figure to the right of the decimal point, the fraction is always read as "tenths." If there are two figures, the fraction is read as "hundredths," and if there are three, it is read as "thousandths." In other words, decimal fractions follow the same progression as do whole numbers, where the first digit is in the "tens" column, the second in the "hundreds," and so forth. As examples, the decimal 0.075 is read as "seventy-five thousandths," and the fraction 0.3852 as "three thousand, eight hundred fifty-two ten-thousandths."

In common fractions, any number may be a denominator. But in decimals, the unwritten denominator is always 10, or some power of 10 such as 100, 1,000, 10,000, and so on. This means that it is simple to change a decimal fraction into a common fraction by putting the proper denominator under the number to the right of the decimal point. Thus, 0.85 becomes the common fraction $^{85}/_{100}$.

To change a common fraction into a decimal, one must divide the numerator by the denominator. In this way, $^3/_4$ can be changed into the decimal 0.75. Not all common fractions, however, can be changed into such precise decimals: $^2/_3$ as a decimal is an endless series of sixes to the right of the decimal point.

TYPES OF COMMON FRACTIONS

There are four kinds of common fractions: proper, improper, mixed, and complex. A

COMPUTING PERCENTAGE

The expression of part of a whole in terms of hundredths is known as percentage. The term "percent" comes from the Latin word *centum*, meaning "hundred." Thus, the whole of something is always 100 percent (100%), or 100 hundredths.

Percentage is closely related to decimal and common fractions. In fact, percentages can be easily changed into both decimal and common fractions, and vice versa. A decimal is changed to a percent by moving the decimal point two places to the right and adding the percentage sign. For example, 0.35 equals 35%. The same procedure is used when there are more than two numbers to the right of the decimal point. Thus, 0.081 becomes 8.1%. A percent is changed to a decimal fraction by dropping the percent sign and moving the decimal point two places to the left. Thus, 85% becomes 0.85 and 4% becomes 0.04.

To change a common fraction to a percent, it is first changed to a decimal with two decimal places (hundredths), and then the decimal to a percent. For example, $1/25 = 0.04 = 4\%$. To change a percent to a common fraction, it is first changed to a decimal. Then the decimal is changed to a common fraction and the fraction is reduced to its lowest terms. For example, $75\% = 0.75 = {}^{75}/_{100} = {}^{3}/_{4}$.

To find a percent of a number, the percent is changed to a decimal fraction and the fraction is multiplied by the number. Thus, 5% of 45 is solved by the equation $0.05 \times 45 = 2.25$.

proper fraction has a numerator smaller than the denominator, such as $^3/_4$. Therefore the value of a proper fraction is always less than one. In improper fractions, the numerator is equal to or larger than the denominator, as $^4/_4$ or $^6/_5$. Thus all improper fractions are equal to or larger than one.

A mixed fraction, also called a mixed number, consists of a whole number and a fraction, such as $2\ ^1/_3$. Any mixed fraction can be changed into an improper fraction by multiplying the whole number by the denominator, adding the result to the numerator, and placing the total over the original denominator. In this way $2\ ^1/_3$ can be changed into $^7/_3$.

Complex fractions, used in higher mathematics, do not consist of natural numbers. For instance, the square root of two over the square root of five is considered a complex fraction:

$$\frac{\sqrt{2}}{\sqrt{5}}$$

Similarly, the use of mixed fractions for both numerator and denominator would create a complex fraction:

$$\frac{2\frac{1}{3}}{3\frac{3}{5}}$$

MIXED NUMBERS

Mixed decimals, known as decimal mixed numbers, occur if a number has figures both to the left and to the right of the decimal point. The number 2.38 is an example: it is read as "two and thirty-eight hundredths." The word "and" is used only where the decimal point appears in order to separate the whole number from the decimal fraction. To avoid confusion, the normal practice for reading decimals is to say "point" instead of "and." The number 2.38 would be read "two point three eight."

There cannot be improper decimal fractions because no numerator (decimal number) could ever exceed the understood denominator (tenths, hundredths, and so on). Anything larger than a decimal fraction would be a mixed or a whole number. Nor would it be possible to express a complex fraction as a decimal with any precision.

COMPUTING WITH FRACTIONS

I t is possible to add, subtract, multiply, and divide with fractions just as with whole numbers. This chapter will be dedicated to techniques for carrying out these operations, first with decimal fractions, then with common fractions. Important rules and examples are also given to help reinforce the lessons.

COMPUTING WITH DECIMAL FRACTIONS

These operations are more easily done with decimals because the procedures are quite similar to using whole numbers. The difference comes in remembering the right placement of the decimal point. It must also be noted that in addition or subtraction, each of the numbers must have the same number of decimal places. To add or subtract uneven decimals, zeros may have to be added to one of the numbers. For instance, to add 3.68 to 7.5, it would be necessary to put a zero at the end of the second decimal to make it 7.50. And in adding or subtracting, the decimal points must always be in a straight column. To perform this addition the numbers should be written thus:

$$
\begin{array}{r}
7.50 \\
+3.68 \\
\hline
11.18
\end{array}
\qquad \text{and not} \qquad
\begin{array}{r}
7.5 \\
+3.68 \\
\hline
\end{array}
$$

The same principles apply when subtracting decimals, and the operation is identical to subtracting whole numbers, except for the presence of the decimal point. If the above problem were to be done as subtraction, it would appear in the same way; only the result would be different:

$$
\begin{array}{r}
7.50 \\
-3.68 \\
\hline
3.82
\end{array}
$$

Notice that the zero must be placed at the end of 7.5 so there is something from which to subtract the 8.

Multiplying with decimals is no more difficult than with whole numbers, except for remembering the correct placement of the decimal point. The chief difference from addition and subtraction is that zeros do not have to be added to fill out a decimal fraction. This is because the adding of zeros might well confuse the placement of the decimal point.

RULES FOR MULTIPLYING WITH DECIMALS

Rule 1. If a decimal is multiplied by a whole number, the number of decimal places in the product is the same as the number of decimal places in the number multiplied.

The problem of multiplying the decimal six–tenths (0.6) by four (4) looks like this:

$$\begin{array}{r} .6 \\ \times 4 \\ \hline \end{array} \quad \text{and the result is} \quad \begin{array}{r} .6 \\ \times 4 \\ \hline 2.4 \end{array} \text{— a mixed decimal}$$

Note that the decimal point is placed before the 4 in the product because there was only one decimal place in the number multiplied (0.6).

Rule 2. If a whole number is multiplied by a decimal, the number of decimal places in the product is the same as the number of decimal places in the multiplier. (Note that this is the reverse of Rule 1 but is exactly the same principle.) To multiply 32 by 2.5, the problem is set up as follows:

$$
\begin{array}{r}
32 \\
\times\,2.5 \\
\end{array}
\quad \text{and the result is} \quad
\begin{array}{r}
32 \\
\times\,2.5 \\
\hline
160 \\
64 \\
\hline
80.0 \\
\end{array}
$$

Note again the placement of the decimal. There was only one decimal place in the multiplier (2.5), therefore only one appears in the product (80.0). In this case, however, the decimal can be eliminated because 80 is a whole number. Had the multiplier been 2.6, the product would have been 83.2, a mixed decimal, and the decimal point would have been retained.

Rule 3. If a decimal is multiplied by a decimal, the number of decimal places in the product is equal to the number of decimal places in the multiplier plus the number of decimal places in the number that is multiplied. If the multiplier and number multiplied together have a total of four decimal places, there will be four decimal places in the product. (Any zeros at the end may, of course, be eliminated.) The problem of multiplying 0.56 by 0.44 is set up as follows:

$$
\begin{array}{r}
.56 \\
\times\,.44 \\
\end{array}
\quad \text{and the result is} \quad
\begin{array}{r}
.56 \\
\times\,.44 \\
\hline
224 \\
224 \\
\hline
.2464 \\
\end{array}
$$

The total shows four decimal places because the multiplier and number multiplied together had four decimal places. In multiplying mixed decimals, the same principle applies. The product of 33.5 × 6.055 is 202.8425, showing four decimal places.

RULES FOR DIVIDING WITH DECIMALS

Rule 1. If a decimal is divided by a whole number, the number of decimal places in the answer is the same as the number of decimal places in the decimal being divided.

Thus, if 0.06 is divided by 2, the answer is 0.03.

Rule 2. When a whole number is divided by a decimal, it is necessary first to convert the decimal to a whole number by moving the decimal point to the right. The decimal point in the number being divided must then be moved the same number of places to the right and zeros added as necessary. The decimal point in the answer is then placed directly above the decimal point in the number being divided:

$$.08\overline{\smash{)}5.00} \text{ becomes } .08\overline{\smash{)}5.000}^{\,62.5}$$

Rule 3. In dividing a decimal by a decimal, the number being divided by is again converted to a whole number, with the decimal point in the number being divided and the decimal point in the answer moved accordingly. Therefore, the answer obtained from dividing 6.816 by 2.13 is 3.2, with one decimal place, obtained by following this rule.

There are certain rules to follow in multiplying with decimals that aid in correct placement of the decimal point.

The process of dividing with decimals is the same as with whole numbers, but it is necessary to be especially careful of decimal point placement. In division there is one main point to remember: the placement of the decimal point in the answer is determined by the placement of the decimal point in the number being divided. As in multiplication, certain rules are helpful.

COMPUTING WITH COMMON FRACTIONS

This procedure is somewhat more complex than with decimals. But it can be simplified if one remembers to make all the fractions have the same denominator. This can be done easily because dividing or multiplying both terms of a fraction by the same number does not change its value. Therefore, to add $2/3$ and $3/4$, it is necessary to find a common denominator. In this case it is 12. The problem becomes $8/12 + 9/12$. The result is found by adding the numerators (8 + 9) to get $17/12$. This answer can be changed to a mixed fraction or a decimal.

The process for subtraction is similar. Find the common denominator, then subtract one numerator from the other:

$$3/4 - 2/3 \text{ becomes } 9/12 - 8/12 = 1/12$$

When dealing with mixed fractions, such as $2\frac{1}{3} + 3\frac{3}{4}$, change them into improper fractions:

Then find the common denominator:

$$7/3 + 15/4$$

This can be changed back to a mixed fraction or to a decimal (6 $\frac{1}{12}$, or a bit over 6.08).

$$28/12 + 45/12 = 73/12$$

In multiplying fractions, both the numerator and the denominator are multiplied. But it is not necessary to find the common denominator. To multiply $\frac{3}{5}$ by $\frac{2}{3}$, multiply the two numerators (3 and 2) to get 6, then the two denominators (5 and 3) to get 15. The answer is $\frac{6}{15}$. This can be reduced to $\frac{2}{5}$, which has the same value, by dividing both terms by 3. Mixed fractions again must be changed to improper fractions before multiplying.

Division with fractions is always done as a multiplication. When any whole number, mixed fraction, or proper fraction is divided by another fraction, that fraction (the divisor) is inverted. Then the two numbers are multiplied as explained in the text above. To divide $^3/_8$ by $^3/_4$, invert the divisor ($^3/_4$) to get $^4/_3$; then multiply to get $^{12}/_{24}$, which can be reduced to $^1/_2$.

If a whole number is divided by a fraction, the fraction is inverted, and the whole number is multiplied by the numerator:

$2 \div 2/3$ becomes $2 \times 3/2 = 6/2$, which is reduced to 3.

Mixed fractions must, of course, be changed to improper fractions:

$4\frac{1}{2} \div 1\frac{1}{2}$ becomes $9/2 \div 3/2$,
then $9/2 \times 2/3 = 18/6$, which reduces to 3.

One result of studying the math history in this book is that our understanding of number systems in the past has now become sharper, its colors richer. The thought that the ancient Mesopotamians used a 360-day year with added months on certain leap years gives pause for thought when the reader considers the later refined year of 365 days with a leap day added every fourth year.

Some of the math inventions of the ancients even remain just as they were used in years past. We still rely on an hour divided into 60 minutes, and a minute divided into 60 seconds, both of which were Mesopotamian creations.

With the mathematics history presented here the reader can ponder where the human race has been and then see how incremental refinements have taken it forward. We gain a sense of comfort with change, an appreciation for how past mathematicians used the information available to measure as best they could, and how with time, number systems were improved to launch humanity into the modern age.

Of course, contemporary times will also change. Math will advance, and currently used number systems will be tweaked and revised to give the world even better mathematical applications, those that yet lie undiscovered.

Glossary

abacus An instrument for making calculations by sliding counters along rods or in grooves.

additive system of numeration Also called sign-value notation, a system for writing numbers in which the value of each numeral is determined by calculating the sum of its individual numeric signs or digits.

algebra A branch of mathematics that uses letters to represent numbers and that studies numbers and the operations (as multiplication and addition) that are used on them.

arithmetic A branch of mathematics that deals with real numbers and their addition, subtraction, multiplication, and division.

base An arbitrarily chosen whole number greater than 1 in terms of which any number can be expressed as a sum of that base raised to various powers.

binary system A system of numbers having two as its base.

common fraction A fraction written as $^a/_b$ that expresses a ratio, or the relationship of one quantity (a) to another (b).

decimal fraction A fraction based on the decimal system in which the unwritten denominator is always 10 or some power of 10 such as 100, 1,000, 10,000, and so on.

decimal system A system of numbers that uses a base of 10.

denominator The part of a fraction that is below the line and that functions as the divisor of the numerator.

digit One of the elements that are used to form numbers in a system; in the decimal system they are any of the Hindu-Arabic numerals 1 to 9 and usually the symbol 0.

duodecimal system Of, relating to, or being a system of numbers with a base of 12.

exponent A symbol written above and to the right of a mathematical expression to mean raising that expression to the power of the symbol.

fraction A number (as $^1/_2$, $^3/_4$, or 3.323) that represents a number of equal parts of a whole or the division of one number by another.

hieroglyphics A system of writing mainly in pictorial characters, especially the picture script of the ancient Egyptians.

irrational number A number (as $\sqrt{2}$) that cannot be expressed as the quotient of two whole numbers.

numeral system A group of symbols representing numbers.

numerator The part of a fraction that is above the line and signifies the number to be divided by the denominator.

positional system of numeration Also called place-value notation, a system for writing numbers in which the value assigned to a digit depends upon its position in the numeral.

quinary system A system of numbers having five as its base.

quotient The number resulting from the division of one number by another.

rational number A number that can be expressed as a whole number or the quotient of two whole numbers.

real number A number (as -2, 3, $^7/_8$, .25, 12, π) that is rational or irrational.

resultant The single vector, or quantity with magnitude and direction, that is the sum of a given set of vectors.

whole number A number that is a natural number (as 1, 2, or 3), the negative of a natural number, or 0.

Academic Games Leagues of America (AGLOA)
P.O. Box 17563
West Palm Beach, FL 33416
(561) 624-1884
Website: http://agloa.org
AGLOA is a nonprofit academic organization
promoting advanced problem-solving-based
thinking in students throughout the United
States. It hosts interschool competitions
and a national championship tournament
based on a series of language arts–, history-,
and mathematics-based games designed to
promote critical thinking.

American Mathematical Society (AMS)
201 Charles Street
Providence, RI 02904
(800) 321-4AMS
Website: http://www.ams.org
The AMS was founded in 1888 to promote
mathematical research and scholarship for
all ages and levels all over the world. Among
other goals, the AMS seeks to increase the
awareness of mathematics and its relation-
ships to other fields and daily life.

Association for Women in Mathematics (AWM)
11240 Waples Mill Road

Suite 200
Fairfax, VA 22030
(703) 934-0163
E-mail: awm@awm-math.org
Website: http://www.awm-math.org
The nonprofit AWM was founded in 1971. The AWM strives to inspire women and girls to study math as well as to seek careers in the mathematical science fields.

Canadian Mathematical Society (CMS)
209-1725 St. Laurent Boulevard
Ottawa, ON K1G 3V4
Canada
(613) 733-2662
E-mail: office@cms.math.ca
Website: http://cms.math.ca
Originally founded as the Canadian Mathematical Congress in 1945, the focus of the CMS is "to promote and advance the discovery, learning and application of mathematics."

MATHCOUNTS Foundation
1420 King Street
Alexandria, VA 22314
(703) 299-9006
E-mail: info@mathcounts.org

Website: http://mathcounts.org

The MATHCOUNTS Foundation is a
nonprofit organization that strives to
encourage middle school students to
view math as fun and challenging. It seeks
to broaden their mathematical oppor-
tunities in school as well as in future
professional lives.

Mathematical Staircase, Inc.
278 Bay Road
Hadley, MA 01035
Website: http://www.mathstaircase.org

Mathematical Staircase, Inc., is a nonprofit
organization whose goal is to provide educa-
tion for mathematically inclined students,
especially those who would otherwise lack
the resources to do so.

Mu Alpha Theta
c/o University of Oklahoma
3200 Marshall Avenue, Suite 190
Norman, OK 73019
(405) 325-4489
Website: http://www.mualphatheta.org

This national high school and two-year col-
lege mathematics honor society has nearly

one hundred thousand members and is involved in over two thousand schools across the United States. Its goal is to develop interest and scholarship in the field of mathematics.

WEBSITES

Because of the changing nature of Internet links, Rosen Publishing has developed an online list of websites related to the subject of this book. This site is updated regularly. Please use this link to access this list:

http://www.rosenlinks.com/TSOM/Numb

For Further Reading

Bentley, Peter J. *The Book of Numbers: The Secret of Numbers and How They Changed the World*. Buffalo, NY: Firefly Books, 2008.

Caron, Lucille, and Philip M. St. Jacques. *Fraction and Decimal Smarts!* (Math Smarts!). Berkeley Heights, NJ: Enslow Publishers, 2011.

Cummings, Alyece B. *Painless Fractions*. 3rd ed. Hauppauge, NY: Barron's Educational Series, 2012.

Fitzgerald, Theresa R. *Math Dictionary for Kids: The Essential Guide to Math Terms, Strategies, and Tables*. 4th ed. Waco, TX: Prufrock Press, 2014.

Frary, Mark. *Mathematics Explained* (The Guide for Curious Minds). New York, NY: Rosen Publishing, 2014.

Higgins, Peter. *Numbers: A Very Short Introduction*. New York, NY: Oxford University Press, 2011.

Higgins, Peter M. *Number Story: From Counting to Cryptography*. Philadelphia, PA: Copernicus Books, 2008.

Hosch, William. *The Britannica Guide to Numbers and Measurements* (Math Explained). New York, NY: Britannica Educational Publishing, 2011.

Reimer, David. *Count Like an Egyptian: A Hands-On Introduction to Ancient Mathematics.* Princeton, NJ: Princeton University Press, 2014.

Rogers, Kirsteen, and Tori Large. *The Usborne Illustrated Dictionary of Math.* London, England: Usborne Publishing, 2009.